AUTOMOTIVE PAINT HANDBOOK

Paint Technology For Auto Enthusiasts & Body Shop Professionals

John Pfanstiehl

HPBooks

HPBooks
Published by
The Berkley Publishing Group
A division of Penguin Putnam Inc.
375 Hudson Street
New York, New York 10014

First edition: August 1998

© 1998 John Pfansthiehl
10 9 8 7 6 5

Library of Congress Cataloging-in-Publication Data

Pfanstiehl, John.
    Automotive paint handbook : paint technology for auto enthusiasts
and body shop professionals / John Pfanstiehl. — Rev. ed.
        p.   cm.
    ISBN 1-55788-291-6
    1. Automobiles—Painting—Handbooks, manuals, etc.   I. Title.
TL255.2.P49   1998   97-45785
629.2'6—dc21   CIP

Cover Design by Bird Studios
Book Design & Production by Michael Lutfy
Interior photos by the author unless otherwise noted
Cover photo courtesy DuPont, Inc.